how to write your first C.V.

SUSAN STOYELL AND LESLEEN EDWARDS

foulsham
LONDON • NEW YORK • TORONTO • SYDNEY

foulsham

The Publishing House, Bennetts Close, Cippenham,
Slough, Berkshire, SL1 5AP, England

ISBN 0-572-02724-9

Printed in Great Britain by the Bath Press, Bath

write
your first
C.V.

Contents

You have decided that the time is right to set out into the world of work, on your road to independence. You are going to look for a job.

Job-hunting means you must go through an active cycle of stages and the easiest way to find your way through those stages is in simple, logical steps – and that's exactly how this book is organised. It's not difficult, but you do need to understand the process in order to make it work to your advantage.

You will probably start by looking at employers who have vacancies that suit you. They may be for an apprentice electrician, a trainee computer operator, a junior secretary or a graduate electronics engineer. These are all opportunities for someone looking for their first job. But there is something else you should be considering: what are they looking for in the applicants who apply?

Quite simply, they want someone who has the level of knowledge required to do the job. They are also looking for the right personality to fit in with the company style and personnel, and a recognisable potential that can be developed.

You have to show them that you have that knowledge, that personality and that potential.

If that sounds daunting, don't worry. By working through this book, step by step, you will learn how to assess all the various aspects of your own knowledge and experience and display them in the best possible light. You will learn to be objective about your positive qualities, and to think about your potential, how you want to use it and how you can demonstrate it to prospective employers.

This is the first step towards a whole new lifestyle for you, as a member of the workforce. There's a lot to think about, find out about and do if you are going to put yourself on the right road – so let's make a start.

There are so many opportunities and options in front of you, you are probably wondering where to start. Don't be put off by the sheer enormity of choices. The trick is to get everything in order and then look at what is best for you. To do this, you are going to have to write a few lists. So think positive and get out paper and pen. The first lists are going to be about you.

Here's looking at you

Take a separate sheet for each list and write down as much as you can under each heading. Remember to be positive.

Personal strengths and qualities

First, think about what sort of aptitudes you have, what your best personal qualities are, and where your strengths lie. Write them down – only the positive ones. Look at the suggestions below and tick those you think are most appropriate to you. Add to the list any others you think are relevant to you.

- [ ] Self-motivated
- [ ] Organised
- [ ] Adaptable
- [ ] Responsible
- [ ] Creative
- [ ] Hard-working
- [ ] Reliable
- [ ] Willing to learn
- [ ] Honest
- [ ] Pay close attention to detail

☐ Work well under pressure

☐ Good at dealing with people

☐ Confident and helpful

☐ Good sense of humour

☐ Good communication skills

☐ Diplomatic

☐ Enthusiastic

☐ Good organisational skills

Ask yourself what you have to offer – everyone has something an employer will want. You have to ask yourself what it is that you have, so that you can tell them. Again, remember to be positive. Form a picture of yourself as a whole, individual person. Put your ideas and conclusions down on paper in list form as before.

Your education and qualifications

Think about your education: list the subjects you have studied, and put them into an order that indicates where you have achieved your best results. Set them down under headings like this:

EXAMINATION (E.G. GCSE, GNVQ, A–LEVEL)	SUBJECT	GRADE

Next, list any examinations you will be taking soon and your estimated grades, again under these headings.

EXAMINATION	SUBJECT	ESTIMATED GRADE

Extra-curricular activities

List the extra-curricular activities that you have most enjoyed at school and college or university: everything from the after-school drama club and sports events to the computer club.

Hobbies, interests and achievements

Write down all your hobbies and activities outside your academic environment: horse riding, helping at a youth club, playing rugby for a local team. Include anything that shows achievement, responsibility or a new experience. If you have spent a period travelling, include that in this list. It will show initiative and experience of different situations and people. Finally, list any certificates or awards you have received for non-academic achievements, such as sports awards, cadet training and a driving licence. Put them under headings something like this:

ACHIEVEMENT	DETAILS

Work experience

List any paid or voluntary work experience that you've had. Don't worry if it is not totally relevant to the kind of jobs or career opportunities you are considering – it will still be of interest to a prospective employer. Write down any comments you have on your experience of the daily pattern of work. Include any tasks that had to be completed to a required standard, any instances of instructions that had to be followed accurately, and areas where you increased your confidence or ability. Put everything under headings.

EMPLOYER	DATE	TYPE OF WORK

Take a harder look at yourself

You need a little more information about yourself in order to establish what sort of job you should be looking for. The sort of job you will do best is one that involves things that you are good at and that you enjoy. So ask yourself a few questions.

What am I most qualified to do?

An easy one, this. Look at your list of qualifications and experience and write down those areas of work you think match your abilities.

What sort of job do I want?

Think about the type of work that you would like to do. Tick any on this list that you would enjoy.

- [ ] Office work
- [ ] Construction/building work
- [ ] Technical/engineering work
- [ ] Art/design
- [ ] Working with people
- [ ] Working with animals
- [ ] Research
- [ ] Creative/working with your hands
- [ ] Management/administration
- [ ] Working with numbers

What do I like doing?

Take a look at the list below and tick those areas or subjects that appeal to you.

☐ Taking responsibility

☐ Organising things

☐ Being part of a team

☐ Leading a team

☐ Working against time/competing against the clock

☐ Being out of doors most of the time

☐ Being indoors most of the time

☐ Learning new skills

☐ Working in a large group or class

☐ Working in a small group or class

☐ Problem-solving activities

☐ Creative activities

☐ Practical activities

☐ Working with old people

☐ Working with young people

☐ Studying

☐ Reading factual information

☐ Reading fiction

☐ Being entertained

☐ Entertaining others

☐ Socialising with people you know

☐ Meeting new people

☐ Being with your family

☐ Dancing

☐ Listening to music

☐ Playing an instrument

☐ Singing

☐ Debating current affairs

☐ Reading national newspapers

☐ Watching news programmes on TV

☐ Watching TV documentaries

☐ Organising your finances

☐ Dressing smartly

☐ Wearing casual clothes

☐ Travelling to new places

☐ Driving

What's important to me?

Think about the kind of job you want. Try to establish if you have any specific career aims or objectives. You also need to think whether there are any organisations you would not work for.

Tick the things that you feel are important to you and should be a priority in your decision-making.

☐ Job security

☐ Varied duties

☐ Routine

☐ Opportunities for further training

☐ Opportunities for promotion

☐ Comfortable working environment

☐ Proximity to home

☐ Good starting salary

☐ Opportunities for progression through training

   and development

☐ A large company

☐ A small company

☐ Social club

☐ Sports amenities

☐ A mainly young workforce

☐ A mixed-age workforce

How do I rate myself?

Make an honest personal assessment of your abilities in
various areas. Give yourself a score between 1 and 10:

0	=	no experience
1–3	=	poor
4–5	=	average
6–7	=	good
8–9	=	very good
10	=	excellent

☐ Practical skills

☐ Creative ability

☐ Ability to analyse

☐ Ability to organise

☐ Ability to communicate in speech

☐ Ability to communicate in writing

☐ Working within a team

☐ Leading others

☐ Organising yourself

☐ Adaptability

☐ Concentration

☐ Learning new skills

☐ Reliability

Looking at the results

Now list all the positive information you have gathered under the major headings as shown.

My best subjects

LIST THE SUBJECTS YOU RATED BEST ON PAGE 10

Things I know I like from experience

LIST THE POSITIVE THINGS YOU TICKED ON PAGE 13

Things that are important to me

LIST THE THINGS YOU TICKED ON PAGE 16

My personal rating

LIST THE SKILLS YOU RATED ON PAGE 16, STARTING WITH THE ONE YOU DO BEST

Discuss the profile you have created with people you know well – your parents, friends, teachers and careers advisers. You should now be forming a clearer picture of your strengths, interests and ambitions, and perhaps some interesting career options may be emerging in your mind.

So let's take the next step and see where and how you can find out more about the career options open to you.

There is a tremendous range of information and sources of help available – and you can't start getting it together too soon. The area you live in and the current state of the job market, both local and national, may affect your choice of job, as well as the personal qualities and experience you have. You need to use all the sources of both information and help you can find, to give you a feel for the opportunities available to you.

Sources of information

College tutors and advisers

If you are still at school or college, start by talking to your tutors and careers advisers. These people should provide plenty of ideas and insight into the work and academic qualifications required in the careers that you think are of interest to you. They will be able to tell you some of your options – and how and where your potential can be used.

Public libraries

You will find masses of careers information in the lending and reference sections and there is always a librarian who will give you a few helpful tips on where to start looking.

Bookshops

You may want to buy some books that you feel are particularly useful. Get together with some friends who are looking at the job market and share the cost. Don't be afraid to ask the bookshop staff for help.

Local and national newspapers

Study the 'Situations Vacant' columns and cut out any advertisements that look interesting, even if it's not the time to put in applications. You may also find feature articles on particular companies or industries that appeal to you. All this information can be used later when you get to the application stage.

The web

Advances in computer technology in the workplace have meant that most employers now advertise and/or promote their organisation on the internet. Surfing the net whilst targeting your specific area of interest will give you a feel for the opportunities available, the qualifications required and often any training available. If you are targeting a specific organisation or market sector, it will also build up background knowledge on your chosen area of work.

Periodicals and trade papers

This is another way to get a 'feel' for an industry that interests you and the career opportunities it offers. You will find many such specialist publications available at your local library.

Directories

These are useful sources of information if you are writing speculatively to companies, i.e. applying for a vacancy when the company or organisation is not actually advertising for anyone. Try:

◆ Kompass directories. These are particularly useful as they cover the UK and give detailed information on the companies listed, the location of which is clearly divided into counties and towns.

◆ Local directories. You will usually find that a local directory or list of local companies is available from your library or council offices.

◆ Yellow Pages. The most obvious of all, especially if you are looking for a local job, as you probably have a copy at home.

Other people

Relatives and friends are usually only too pleased to add to your careers information bank. Find out what they do and how they feel about their work. Do they have any contacts in the industries that you are considering?

Keeping the information together

Be businesslike in the way you compile and keep information. Start a folder where you can keep your personal profile, all your advertisements, press cuttings and notes.

Also keep a record of what you have done, something like this:

Speak to

◆ Careers adviser/tutor

◆ Relatives

◆ Friends

Check other sources

◆ Libraries

◆ Careers books

◆ Local papers

◆ The web

◆ National newspapers

◆ Periodicals/trade journals

◆ Directories

Start a careers folder

Having compiled a lot of information on your options, keep your mind clear by writing down, in order of preference, the careers that interest you most.

Referring back to the personal profile you put together on page 17, you should find that your qualifications, strengths, likes and ambitions are matching up to the probable requirements of the kind of job you are looking for.

If you have a problem relating and matching them, now is the time to re-think your ideas and explore other career possibilities. This can stop you venturing up some blind alleys.

Remember: somewhere there will always be an employer who wants the potential you have to offer.

You should now have a file full of career facts, a list of attractive possible careers/jobs and a realistic self-appraisal. Now is the time to demonstrate your potential, get your personal job-search campaign together, and show them what you have to offer. This will all be put together in your CV, or resumé, as it is sometimes known. CV stands for the Latin expression *curriculum vitae,* meaning 'the course of one's life', so it is just a summary of your career history to date.

A good CV

A good CV is the first stage in your career or job search, and it will be a key step to winning a job offer. It is the one that gets you that interview for the job you want. An effective CV should:

◆ Create a good impression of your aims and ability

◆ Present your relevant skills, knowledge and qualities clearly and concisely

◆ Give a good overall view of you

Your CV needs to give the facts about you in a clear and presentable way, so that it captures and holds the interest of the reader and makes them want to meet you.

A prospective employer will be looking for information that will tell them that the writer of this CV has:

◆ The skills, knowledge or commitment to do the job on offer

◆ Experience or at least some knowledge or interest relevant to the job

◆ Experience of similar challenges or experience in the past

◆ The personal qualities to do the job and/or to fit into a team

Guidelines to writing your CV

Your CV should be simple, concise and positive. A job advertisement can attract a large number of replies and reading CVs can become an onerous task for the most conscientious employer.

Keep it short, no more than two pages. Make it easy to read. It should be typed, spell-checked and laid out in a logical order. Keep the information relevant. Use positive words and phrases. Divide it into sections under separate headings.

Areas to cover

- Personal details
- Personal statement
- Career objectives
- Work experience
- Education and qualifications
- Responsibilities and offices held at school, college, university
- Non-academic achievements
- Leisure interests
- Referees

Presentation

Make the whole thing look as professional as possible.

- Use plain white or cream A4 paper.
- Use black, not coloured, ink.
- Avoid alterations and amendments. If you make a mistake, start again. Do not send poor-quality photocopies.
- Do not include photographs, unless they are requested.

Suggested CV layout

Your CV should run something like this.

Personal details

Name: Give your first names before your surname, e.g. Janet Amanda Jones.

Address: Give your full address and include your postcode.

Telephone number: Include your area code and indicate if you can be contacted during the day or evenings only. (If you have an answerphone, make sure that the message on it is business-like. A company may phone in response to your application and your message will form their first impression of you, so it would probably be wise to get rid of any disco music or jokey voices you may have on it.)

E-mail address: Include this, if you have one.

Personal profile

This is a very important part of your CV and in some ways is the most difficult to write. It is here that you should lay out your skills, knowledge, experience, capabilities, strengths and achievements. If you have previous work experience, you can draw on that. Otherwise, try to present everything about you that is relevant to the job you are applying for. Divide it into a summary of three areas:

◆ Your personal characteristics, your qualities, ability and to some extent your personality. You can give information on areas which are not apparent from the rest of your CV, e.g. that you work well under pressure, are creative and adaptable, good at motivating and directing, enjoy new challenges, etc.

◆ A career profile highlighting specific achievements and skills attained to date (if you have them), e.g. a thorough understanding of book-keeping systems; excellent language skills developed through teaching students in a foreign country, etc.

◆ A summary of your career objectives, i.e. the type of position you are aiming at. (If you are making a speculative approach to a company it can help them to have an idea what you are looking for.)

If you are replying to a job advertisement, study the wording: the key requirements for the successful candidate will have been included in it, and you should use this information when writing your CV. It is essential that you make sure that the essence of the job title and description are reflected in your statement. So if they say they are looking for someone with experience in research, or with excellent interpersonal skills, make sure that you mention in your personal profile statement that you have such knowledge and experience and want to use them.

Use phrases such as 'proven administrative skills, with specific experience in'; 'an experienced driver'; 'a fully trained animal handler with experience of...'; 'able to communicate at all levels' and 'a keen interest in...'.

Use words that describe personal qualities which can be positive and helpful in the workplace, such as adaptable, analytical, articulate, assertive, creative, decisive, dependable, efficient, energetic, enthusiastic, friendly, hardworking, imaginative, motivated, objective, organised, outgoing, quick-thinking, self-motivated, smart, versatile, willing.

To sum up:

◆ Identify what they want.

◆ Consider what you have to offer (think positive!).

◆ Match the two as closely as possible.

Career objectives

Go back to your self-assessment exercises in Step 1 and look at what you wrote under 'What's important to me?'. If you were quite specific about the type of job you are looking for, then you can be precise in stating your given objectives here on your CV. If you want to keep your options open and apply for several different types of job, then keep it general or leave it out.

Example of specific career objective

I feel that I have the potential to develop a successful career in accountancy and I would like to work for a company that can offer me the necessary opportunity and, I hope, the assistance to further my studies towards a professional qualification.

Example of general objective

I am keen to find a progressive position with a company that can offer me training and the scope to develop a successful career.

Career history

List the organisations or companies you have worked for starting with the most recent, as that is the most relevant. Make sure you give all the following information:

◆ Company name

◆ Dates (e.g. October 1998–March 2001)

◆ Job title

◆ Brief description of what you did and any achievements

Work experience

If you are a school-leaver or have just finished college, you may not have any career history but you will probably have had some casual work experience. Give full details of it here – dates, the name of your employer and what your job was. For instance:

JUNE–SEPTEMBER 2001 (SUMMER HOLIDAYS)	JC SMITH AND SONS	PACKER
DECEMBER 1988 (CHRISTMAS HOLIDAYS)	THE POST OFFICE	POST SORTER

Education

Name your school(s), college and/or university. Include the dates when you attended, arranging them with the most recent first. Don't go back further than secondary school.

For example:

1997–2000	SOMETHING UNIVERSITY, KING STREET, NEWTOWN, KENT
1995–1997	SOMETHING SIXTH FORM COLLEGE, HIGH STREET, HIGH TOWN, SURREY
1991–1995	SOMETHING SECONDARY SCHOOL, HIGH STREET, MIDDLEWITCH, SANDWICH, KENT

Qualifications achieved

List the examinations you have taken and passed and those where you are awaiting results. Give the highest grades first. They should be arranged something like this:

GCSE	
SUBJECT	GRADE
(LIST THEM ALL)	
A-LEVEL	
SUBJECT	GRADE
(LIST THEM ALL)	
GNVQ	
SUBJECT	ESTIMATED GRADE (AWAITING RESULT)

Note: Do not supply some grades and not others. If the grades are not good, leave them all out and just give subjects passed.

If you are a graduate, a synopsis of the content of your degree course can be included, but only if it is relevant to the application.

Responsibilities and offices held at school, college or university

Give details of anything you have done that shows you have been put in a position of trust or responsibility. For instance:

◆ Captain of the First XI cricket team

◆ Member of chess club

◆ Head girl/boy

◆ Officer in CCF

◆ Chairman of college debating society

Remember: Avoid anything that shows a strong party political bias, unless, of course, you are looking for a career in politics.

Non-academic achievements

If you have achieved a certificate, trophy or award of some kind, list those in this section. Where appropriate, give the name of the body that awarded the certificate. For instance:

- 5,000 metre certificate for swimming (International STA Distance Award)
- Green belt for judo
- Grade V1 certificate for ballet (Royal Academy of Dancing)
- Duke of Edinburgh bronze/silver/gold medal

Leisure interests

Give four or five of your favourite hobbies and try to provide a good mix that shows you in both 'switched-on' and 'switched-off' mode. Strike a good balance between the physically active and more intellectual pursuits.

Do not put something down that you know little about – you could easily be caught out if asked to talk about it at an interview (so if you put down 'reading', be prepared to discuss your favourite authors). An example of a good mix would be:

- Keep-fit activities, such as yoga, kick-boxing, dance, running, cricket, squash, football, riding, swimming, etc.
- Listening/playing music (you can identify the type if you wish: pop, classical, folk, country, etc.)
- Active member of a conservation society, wildlife organisation
- Reading, any kind of collection (e.g. stamps), photography

Professional training

List any courses you have attended. Give the dates, qualification, skills and knowledge gained.

Personal details

Date of birth/age: Use a simple form, e.g. 25 October 1981, followed by your age in brackets.

Nationality: Only include this if it has been requested in the advertisement. Use 'British', not 'English' or 'Welsh', etc.

Marital status: It is not necessary to include this, unless you wish to do so. Employers nowadays do not usually ask about this.

Driving licence: If relevant to the job (e.g. van driver, sales representative), give the type of licence you hold – clean, full, provisional, motorcycle and/or car, HGV. If you own a vehicle, then add this in brackets.

Health: Be brief and give only necessary information

Smoker/non-smoker: As most companies have restricted smoking facilities, it can be helpful to state if you are a non-smoker. If you do smoke, leave it out!

References

You should be prepared to provide the names and addresses of two referees (make sure that you have asked them first). One could be the headteacher of the last school or college you attended. The other should be a personal referee – if possible, someone who holds a position of authority and status and who knows you quite well. Someone who has employed you during weekends or holiday periods would be ideal. However, it is quite acceptable to say, 'References will be available on request'.

Photographs

These are usually unnecessary and should not be included unless specifically requested as part of the application. If you are asked to send one, choose a head and shoulders portrait (not a holiday snap) and affix it to your letter of application.

Checklist

Once you have prepared your draft, check it to see whether it contains the essentials listed on page 24.

In addition, ask yourself:

◆ Is it written clearly – preferably typed – on A4 paper?

◆ Have you checked the spelling?

◆ Is it the right length?

◆ Is it arranged in easy-to-read sections?

◆ Does it present a positive picture of you?

◆ Are your skills, knowledge, experience and achievements clearly described?

◆ Is it free of irrelevant details?

◆ Is it businesslike in its presentation?

◆ Are the dates you have given correct?

◆ Have you asked your chosen referees if they are agreeable to being contacted?

If you are satisfied that the answers to all of these questions are 'Yes', have your CV photocopied. This can be done at most post offices and libraries for a small charge, usually around 10p per sheet. Keep your copied CVs in a box or folder so that they are flat, crisp and clean.

CV examples

On pages 32–41 are examples of five CVs that will make the reader want to meet you and encourage them to give you an interview. In each case, the applicants are presenting themselves to take full advantage of their individual qualifications, achievements and career objectives.

Example 1

Name: Deborah Freeman

Address: 12 Woodpecker Lane, London, W1 3BA

Telephone number: 020 7983 0356 (evenings)

E-mail address: deborahf@anymail.com

Personal profile

A competent, highly motivated graduate with some experience of the work environment. Quick to learn and used to working under pressure and meeting deadlines. A flexible, practical person trained in analytical methods, seeking a career within an engineering/project management environment.

Education

1998–2001	UNIVERSITY OF SOMETHING
1996–1998	SOMETHING SIXTH FORM COLLEGE, LONDON W11 2XN
1991–1996	SOMETHING SECONDARY SCHOOL, LONDON W1 5TJ

Qualifications

GCSEs:	MATHEMATICS (A), TECHNICAL DRAWING(A), PHYSICS (B), CHEMISTRY (B), GEOGRAPHY (B), ENGLISH LANGUAGE (C), FRENCH (C)
A-LEVELS:	PHYSICS (A), MATHEMATICS (A), CHEMISTRY (B)
DEGREE:	CURRENTLY IN THE FINAL YEAR OF A 3-YEAR BSc DEGREE COURSE IN ENGINEERING SCIENCE

PLEASE SEE DETAILS OF MY DEGREE COURSE ATTACHED.

Work experience

DECEMBER 1999	G ARMITAGE LTD, LONDON	STOCK CONTROLLER
JUNE–SEPTEMBER 1999	G ARMITAGE LTD, LONDON	VDU CLERK (PURCHASING)
DECEMBER 1998	THE POST OFFICE	POSTAL WORKER
JUNE–AUGUST 1998	OAKLEY FARM, SUSSEX	FRUIT PICKER

Non-academic achievements

St John's Ambulance First Aid Certificate

Responsibilities held at school/college/university

Member of college fund-raising committee

Captain of college First X1 hockey team

Stage manager of university 2000 Rag Revue

Leisure interests

Squash, theatre, music (jazz), computing

Personal details

Date of birth: 12 February 1979 (age 22)

Nationality: British

Driving licence: Full, clean (car and motorcycle owner)

Referees

Dr R Hill, Department of Engineering, University of Something

Mr G Townsend, Managing Director, G Armitage Ltd, London NW3 5DX

Example 2

Name: Janet Rowland

Address: Field Gate, High View, Tipton, Sussex, SS1 1SS

Telephone number: 01234 56789 (evenings)

E-mail: rowlandj@wayhay.com

Personal profile

A good communicator who has demonstrated initiative and self-motivation. An outgoing, down-to-earth person with a good sense of humour, who can communicate and fit in well at all levels.

Career objective

I am looking for an opportunity to work in a sales office where I would be trained in general office procedure, come to understand the company's products and eventually be trained for a career in field sales.

Education

1999–2001	SOMETHING COLLEGE, NEW TOWN, SUSSEX
1995–1999	TORINGTON SCHOOL, TORINGTON, SUSSEX

Qualifications

GCSEs: ENGLISH LANGUAGE (A), BIOLOGY (B), MATHEMATICS (B), CHEMISTRY (C), FRENCH (C)

RSA (1): TYPING

A-LEVELS (WITH ESTIMATED GRADES): ENGLISH (B), GEOGRAPHY (C)

Non-academic achievements

CURRENT HOLDER OF THE SOMETHING SHOW-JUMPING JUNIOR NATIONAL CHAMPIONSHIP

Work experience

DECEMBER 1999	THE MOAT HOTEL, TORINGTON, SUSSEX	KITCHEN ASSISTANT
JULY—AUGUST 1999	THE DAILY CHRONICLE, TORINGTON, SUSSEX	MESSENGER

Personal details

DATE OF BIRTH:	20 JANUARY 1983 (AGE 19)
HEALTH:	GOOD, NON-SMOKER
DRIVING LICENCE:	FULL, CLEAN (I INTEND TO BUY A CAR WHEN I START WORK)

Referees

MR C PENN, HEADMASTER, SOMETHING COLLEGE, NEW TOWN, SUSSEX

MR B THORPE, EDITOR, THE DAILY CHRONICLE, TORINGTON, SUSSEX

Example 3

Name: Matthew Gareth Evans

Address: 1 Valley Way, Caernarfon, Gwynedd, GW2 5KB

Telephone number: 01345 67892 (evenings)

Personal profile

I am a practical person and would like to learn a trade. I am seeking an apprenticeship or a job that will allow me to gain skills as I progress. I am hard-working and reliable with an eye for detail and the ability to work accurately to instructions.

Education

1996–2001	SOMETHING SCHOOL, CAERNARFON

Qualifications

(AWAITING RESULTS)

GCSEs (ESTIMATED GRADES): TECHNICAL DRAWING (B), MATHEMATICS (C), BIOLOGY (C), PHYSICS (C), ENGLISH LANGUAGE (C/D)

Non-academic achievements

PLAYED IN SCHOOL FIRST X1 FOOTBALL TEAM

HAVE TAKEN PART IN VARIOUS FUND-RAISING CHARITY WALKS AND SWIMS

Responsibilities/offices held at school

SIXTH-FORM PREFECT

Leisure interests

MOTOR MECHANICS, FOOTBALL, DESIGNING/BUILDING MODEL AEROPLANES

Work experience

JUNE 2001 TO DATE: HIGH STREET NEWSAGENTS, CAERNARFON   NEWSPAPER ROUND

Personal details

DATE OF BIRTH: 12 MAY 1995 (AGE 16)
NATIONALITY: BRITISH
HEALTH: GOOD
DRIVING LICENCE: PROVISIONAL GROUP E (MOPED)

Referees

MR J KING, HEADMASTER, SOMETHING SCHOOL, CAERNARFON, GWYNEDD, GW16 9JU

MRS S DAVIES, MANAGER, HIGH STREET NEWSAGENTS, CAERNARFON, GWYNEDD, GW1 2JR

Example 4

Name: Jishno Rao

Address: 12 King Street, New Town, Lancs, MK20 2JB

Telephone number: 01987 65432 (evenings)
01987 12345 (days)

Personal profile

A highly motivated college leaver with work experience within the hotel and catering industry. A good communicator who enjoys the challenge of a busy and demanding work load.

Career objective

I have enjoyed my BTEC course and have done well. I am now seeking a position as trainee manager in a hotel that is part of a major group, with the opportunity for advancement for the successful candidate.

Work experience

DECEMBER 2000	THE BRIDGE HOTEL, NEW TOWN	KITCHEN HAND/VEGETABLE CHEF
JUNE–AUGUST 2000	THE SWAN HOTEL, NEW TOWN	KITCHEN HAND
DECEMBER 1999	THE BRIDGE HOTEL, NEW TOWN	WAITER
APRIL 1999	THE BRIDGE HOTEL, NEW TOWN	WAITER

Education

1999–2001	SOMETHING COLLEGE, NEW TOWN
1995–1999	SOMETHING SCHOOL, NEW TOWN

Qualifications

GCSEs:	ENGLISH LITERATURE (B), GEOGRAPHY (B), ENGLISH LANGUAGE (C), MATHEMATICS (C), BIOLOGY (C), CHEMISTRY (D)
BTEC NATIONAL DIPLOMA:	HOTEL & CATERING OPERATIONS

Non-academic achievements

DUKE OF EDINBURGH AWARD (BRONZE)

Responsibilities and offices held at school/college

CAPTAIN FIRST X1 SCHOOL CRICKET TEAM

Leisure interests

CRICKET, READING, CHESS

Personal details

DATE OF BIRTH: 20 FEBRUARY 1983 (AGE 18)
NATIONALITY: BRITISH
MARITAL STATUS: SINGLE
HEALTH: GOOD, NON-SMOKER
DRIVING LICENCE: FULL, CLEAN (CAR OWNER)

Referees

MR S JOHNSON, HEADMASTER, SOMETHING COLLEGE, NEW TOWN, LANCS, MK25 7ST

MR C RICHARDS, THE MANAGER, THE BRIDGE HOTEL, NEW TOWN, LANCS, MK20 5ET

Example 5

Name: Jonathon Peter Kirby

Address: The Farm, River Lane, Switcham, Norfolk, IP23 6JD

Telephone number: 01224 667788 (days/evenings)

Personal statement

I am competitive and mentally and physically strong.
I would like to be an apprentice in a successful National
Hunt Stables and prove myself a winning jockey, with the
ultimate ambition of winning the Grand National at least
once in my career.

Education

1996–2001	SOMETHING SCHOOL, SWITCHAM

Work experience

DECEMBER 2000	SOMETHING RIDING SCHOOL	STABLE HAND
JULY–AUGUST 2000	SOMETHING RIDING SCHOOL	STABLE HAND
1997 TO DATE	HILL ROAD NEWSAGENTS	MORNING PAPER ROUND

Qualifications

GCSEs:	BIOLOGY (C), ENGLISH LANGUAGE (C), MATHEMATICS (C)

Non-academic achievements

I HAVE WON A NUMBER OF MEDALS AT INTER-SCHOOL SWIMMING CHAMPIONSHIPS

Responsibilities and offices held at school

PREFECT

Leisure interests

RIDING AND HORSES, FOLLOWING THE RACING NEWS, MOUNTAINEERING

Personal details

DATE OF BIRTH:	6 JUNE 1985 (AGE 16)
HEALTH:	GOOD
WEIGHT:	85 LBS*
DRIVING LICENCE:	FULL, CLEAN. GROUP E (MOPED)

Referees

MR S THOMAS, SOMETHING SCHOOL, SWITCHAM, NORFOLK, IP24 7LN

CAPTAIN R WAINWRIGHT, SOMETHING STABLES, NEWTOWN, NORFOLK, IP20 2NU

*In the case of this particular application, this is an important piece of information.

When you send your CV to a prospective employer, it should always be accompanied by a letter in your own handwriting. The letter should be brief but 'punchy'. Draft it carefully beforehand and think about it until you have it right.

Your address should be written in full (remembering the postcode) at the top right of the paper, followed by the date, also written in full (e.g. 20 January 2001).

Underneath, at the left-hand side, put the name of the person or the title of the person to whom you have been asked to send the application. Underneath that, write the name and address of the company, followed by any reference numbers given in the advertisement.

If the advertisement gave the name of a person to whom the letter and application should be sent, start the letter with his name: 'Dear Mr Smith', for example. If the recipient is a woman and it is not clear whether she is a Mrs or a Miss, use Ms, e.g. 'Dear Ms Smith'. When you are writing to a named person, finish the letter 'Yours sincerely', and sign your name underneath. If the advertisement does not give the name of any particular person to whom the letter is to be sent, start 'Dear Sir/Madam', and finish the letter 'Yours faithfully', followed again by your signature.

Underneath your signature it is a good idea to print your name. Remember:

◆ Use good-quality, plain A4 notepaper.

◆ Use a good pen.

◆ Use black ink.

◆ Keep your lines straight (use a guide sheet underneath if necessary).

◆ Write neatly.

◆ Check your grammar.

◆ Check your spelling.

◆ Make a carbon copy or photocopy to keep in a file together with the job advertisement.

Typical layout of a letter of application

12 The Avenue

New Town

Middlesex

MC2 1LX

20 July 2001

Mr LC Smith

The Personnel Manager

Wyvern Engineering Company Ltd

Saxon Industrial Estate

New Town

Middlesex

MC1 2QY

Ref. AC/221/J

Dear Mr Smith,

Re: Accounts Clerk. Your Advertisement: The Chronicle 19 July 2001

Yours sincerely,

Andrew Fletcher

Wording a letter of application

When you are replying to an advertisement, the right words will not come until you have read and re-read the advertisement and have broken down exactly what it is that has attracted you to the vacancy and why you think you are right for the job. Try doing it this way:

First underline in red the words that caught your eye. These may be:

◆ The company name. It might be a company you know something about – perhaps it's a company in your careers file, you might know people there or they might be situated close to where you live.

◆ The type of business. Its products or services may be something you admire or use.

◆ The job itself. It could be just what you have in mind for yourself.

◆ The location. Perhaps it's situated close to you – or perhaps it offers transport by a company bus.

Hopefully, it will be a combination of several of these factors. Also underline any phrases describing aspects of the job that might be important to you, such as 'international company'; 'multi-million pound turnover'; 'expanding company'; 'part of a major group of companies'; 'excellent prospects'; 'training opportunities'; 'a clean working environment'; 'the UK market leader in …'.

Now underline in blue or black the specified requirements that suit your abilities. They could be:

◆ Education to a particular standard

◆ An analytical mind

◆ Good communication skills

◆ An interest in computers

◆ A bright young person willing to train in …

◆ No experience necessary

◆ A smart appearance

Now look back at your personal assessments (see pages 9–17) and think about the job you are applying for. Decide if and how you fit the bill and whether it satisfies your requirements. If you are clear on these points, the letter will not be a problem.

If all the signs are good, you will be feeling enthusiastic. So let's start writing.

Spelling out your potential

The message you need to get across is 'I am keen, clear, businesslike and sincere'. Use this to divide your letter into four paragraphs.

Paragraph 1: I am keen

Start by making the statement that you are keen on applying for the vacancy.

Paragraph 2: I am clear

Show that you have read the advertisement carefully and have a clear understanding of the job and the company requirements. Say why you think you match their requirements.

Paragraph 3: I am businesslike

Make it easier for the company by saying when you are available for interview and when you will be ready to start work. This can save the company a lot of time when they are trying to make appointments to suit a number of people apart from yourself.

Paragraph 4: I am sincere

Round off the letter by leaving them in no doubt that you are sincerely interested in the job.

Sample letters of application

Let's now look at two examples of advertisements for job you might wish to apply for. In each case, you are going to base the content of your letter on the information you can glean from the advertisement.

Example 1

An effective advertisement such as the one given below tells you all you need to know – the job, what it involves, the type of company they are and the type of person they are looking for.

Junior Administrator

A <u>smart, enthusiastic</u> young person is required to join our <u>energetic sales administration team.</u>

You will be dealing with customer enquiries and orders mostly taken by <u>telephone.</u>

Keystores is one of a multi–branch <u>retail chain</u> specialising in computers.

The prospects are excellent for an <u>ambitious</u> young person with <u>initiative</u> and an <u>interest in computers.</u>

Apply in writing to ...

I have underlined the points that most suitable applicants will find relevant and attractive. Taking these into account, you might apply along the lines of the sample letter overleaf.

There are a number of key words used in this letter.

◆ **Keen** A good positive word

◆ **Believe** Shows confidence in your own judgment

◆ **Ideal** Shows you are attaching importance to finding the right job and not just any old job

◆ **Hope** Reinforces keenness and is a polite, nice way to round off the letter

12 Sun Hill
Uckthorpe
Middlesex
MM2 0LJ
16 June 2001

Miss J Smith
Keystores
2, High Street
Uckthorpe
Middlesex
MM1 6QJ

Dear Miss Smith

Re: Your vacancy for a Junior Administrator, The Daily Chronicle, 15 June 2001

I have read your advertisement for a junior administrator and I am keen to apply. Please find my CV enclosed.

This post would seem to offer an ideal opportunity to combine my interest in computers and my interest in a retailing career, and I believe that I have what it takes to match your requirements.

I am 17 years old and I am interested in fashion and fashion trends. I am reliable, ambitious and enthusiastic, and very willing to learn. I work well in a team and I also like using my initiative. I am confident using the telephone. I have a home computer and enjoy surfing the net.

I leave school on 25 June and I would be available to start work immediately afterwards. If you wish to see me for an interview, I would be pleased to attend any weekday after 4 pm or on a Saturday. After I have left school, I could come at any time.

I hope that you will consider me a good candidate for interview.

Yours sincerely

Paul Page

Example 2

This very short advertisement tells you very little, so it is much more difficult to pick up anything from it to use in your letter. As before, I have underlined points you might find attractive but you will need to build on that information and add to it if you are to write a good letter of application.

ALEXANDER'S <u>HAIR</u> SALON

<u>Junior</u>

Required <u>urgently</u> to join our <u>team.</u> <u>Top</u> <u>wages</u> paid.

Apply in writing to ...

Try to decide what it is that this employer is going to be looking for when they sift through the applications. They are a hairdressing business looking for a junior urgently. That much you know, but what else? Try to look at the situation through the employer's eyes and make some **careful** assumptions.

They are **likely** to be seeking:

◆ Someone with an interest in hair styling

◆ A creative person

◆ Someone with a smart appearance

◆ A hard-working person

◆ Someone who gets on well with people

With all this in mind, you could apply along the lines of the letter on page 50.

10 Cedar Way
Upten
Glos
GL15 9JJ
13 June 2001

Mrs J Brown
Alexander's Hair Salon
5, King Street
Upten
Glos
GL20 6SU

Dear Mrs Brown

Re: Your vacancy for a Junior, The Daily Chronicle 12 June 2001

I have read your advertisement for a junior and I am keen to apply. Please find my CV enclosed.

This vacancy seems an ideal opportunity for me to train with a local and well-established hair salon and I believe that I could make a success with the job.

I enjoy styling my own hair and other people's and I care about my appearance. I get on well with people of all age groups. I am hardworking and reliable, and have a flexible approach to the hours I work. I could start work immediately.

I left school on 28 May and have just come back from my annual holiday. I am hoping to find a job in hairdressing that I can start soon.

If you would like to interview me, I would be pleased to come and see you on any day except next Tuesday.

I hope that you will consider me for the vacancy.

Yours sincerely

Sheila Watson

Speculative applications

You may find a company that you might like to work for, although you do not have any particular reason for thinking that they have a suitable opening. In this case, it is worth making a speculative approach to them – provided you are prepared for disappointment. Having said that, it is surprising how often these long shots pay off.

Whether a company has a vacancy to fill or not, they are always attracted to a speculative approach because it demonstrates energy, courage and enthusiasm in the applicant.

Making the first move

If you're applying to a company in the hope that they will have a position to suit you, the most important thing is to send your letter to a named person, because you can then be sure that the letter will attract their attention and draw a response. To do this, telephone the company and ask for the name and initials of the Human Resources or Personnel Manager. If they do not have such a person, ask for the name of the Manager or the General Manager or Chief Executive. Alternatively, explain what you want to do and ask the company telephone operator if they can give you the name of an appropriate person.

Speculative letters should be brief, spelling out why you are interested in the company, and giving your skills, qualifications and any qualities which you think may be of interest to them. Accompany the letter with your CV.

You may find some companies simply place your letter on file in case a suitable vacancy occurs, so you might not hear anything for quite a long period of time. In fact, you may not hear from them at all. Don't let this discourage you or put you off applying to their advertisements in the future. It may simply mean that their system does not cope well with speculative applications and, to be fair, some companies do receive a lot. However, if you don't get any response, it is safe to assume that there is nothing suitable for you at the moment.

A speculative letter should be written along these lines:

12 Sun Hill
Bedford
MK22 6JJ
20 June 2001

Mr P J Jones
Personnel Manager
Blank Electronics Company Ltd
High View Industrial Estate
Bedford
MK25 6PL

Dear Mr Jones

I am writing to you with my CV enclosed in the hope that you may have a vacancy for a Trainee Electronics Technician.

My qualifications to date are 6 good GCSE passes and I am about to take Physics, Chemistry and Maths A-levels.

I am very keen on Electronics and read as much as possible on the subject by visiting the reference library and looking at trade journals such as Electronics Weekly and Electronics Times. In my leisure time, I enjoy using my computer and have done some programming in BASIC.

If you have a vacancy that might suit me, I would be very pleased to have the opportunity of an interview and could attend any day except for the week commencing 26 June. I would be able to start work after 20 July.

I hope that this application will be of interest to you.

Yours sincerely

John Smith

Check and check again

The examples I have given of application letters are intended as guides only and have been provided to give you a feel of how they should be approached. Remember though, that a good application is a reflection of you, so find your own words and let your enthusiasm and personality shine through.

Keep a copy of each letter you write, together with the advertisement to which you are applying in a file labelled Applications.

Use the checklist given on page 43 when sending speculative letters of application.

You may find that, in an advertisement, you are asked to telephone in or write for a company application form – most companies have their own.

Letter asking for an application form

If you are asked to write, a very brief letter is all that is needed – a longer letter should be sent when you return the application form. Use this sample letter as a guide and personalise it to suit the circumstances.

22 Orchard Drive
Bedford
MK4 2JG
17 August 2001

Miss PJ Jones
Personnel Manager
Blank Electronics Company
High View Estate
Bedford
MK25 6PL

Dear Miss Jones

Re: Your vacancy for a Trainee Electronics Engineer, Daily Chronicle, 16 August 2001

I would like to apply for the vacancy of Trainee Electronics Engineer with your company and I would be grateful if you would send me an application form and job description. I would also be pleased to receive any information concerning your company and their products.

Thank you for your assistance in this matter.

Yours sincerely

Kate Brown

Completing the form

The information provided by company application forms is used in the early stages to decide on the interview shortlist. You will normally be asked to fill it in and return it with your CV attached. Some companies prefer to ask you to complete their application form when you are called for an interview. Alternatively, you may be given one to complete at the second interview stage or even just prior to an offer. It depends on the company's recruitment procedure and there are no hard and fast rules that apply.

At whichever point you have to complete such a form, always tackle it carefully. The degree of care you show in undertaking this sometimes tedious task tells the reader much about you. Note that they usually contain a declaration that the facts you have given about yourself are correct.

Complete the form in black ink (it reproduces better if it has to be photocopied) and avoid crossings-out or smudges. If you are doing it at home or off the company premises, make sure you have a flat, clean surface on which to write.

Read the form well first – as you would an exam paper – and think out your answers before putting pen to paper.

If you are doing it at home, take a copy if you can and practise your answers on it first. If you are instructed to use block capitals, make sure you do, from beginning to end.

Remember to have your CV with you at all times in case you are asked to complete an application form. This will make life a lot easier for you as you will have all the details and factual information covering such things as qualifications, grades and dates ready, checked and correct.

Some company forms can be quite long and complicated. If there are questions that you do not understand, complete as much as you can and then ask someone to explain the remainder.

Do not leave questions unanswered if they do not apply to you. Simply write N/A (this means 'not applicable'). In this way, the reader can see that you have not left out anything by mistake.

You will probably be asked for the following information.

First names: List all your forenames.

Surname: This is your last name or family name.

Mr/Mrs/Ms/Miss: Circle whichever is applicable to you or delete those that are not.

Source of application: They want to know how you heard about the vacancy. If it was a newspaper advertisement, state in which paper you saw it and the date it appeared.

Next of kin: Give the name and address of the person most closely related to you. If you are unmarried, it is likely to be your parent, guardian or partner. If you are married, it will be your husband or wife.

Dependants: Here you should give the names of any people that you are responsible for, such as children.

Application form checklist

- ◆ Read the form carefully.
- ◆ Make sure you understand all the questions.
- ◆ Make sure you note any special instructions, such as using block capitals.
- ◆ Note in which order to enter your names.
- ◆ Use a good pen.
- ◆ Check that any dates/grades given are consistent with those on your CV.
- ◆ Think out your answers to all the questions in advance.
- ◆ Keep the form clean and write on a flat, clean surface.

Completing your application form – right and wrong

Here are a couple of examples of completed application forms.

Example 1 contains some basic, commonly made mistakes. Can you spot them? There are ten in all. You can check them with the answers provided on page 59. In Example 2, James has made a good job of completing the form clearly and fully.

Example 1: The wrong way

Bloggs and Bloggs Limited

Please return this application form to:
The Personnel Department, Bloggs and Bloggs Ltd, Gimchurch, Middlesex
Answer in BLOCK CAPITALS.
Confidential application for employment

Source of application: The Daily Chronicle	Date of application: 20 June 2001

Post applied for: Junior Accounts Clerk

Surname: Mr/~~Mrs/Miss/Ms~~ John Michael Smith

First Name(s):

Address: 25, The Moor, Gimchurch, Middlesex

Telephone number(s): 01765 43219

Date of birth: 1.1.01	Place of birth: Hospital
Nationality: English	Marital Status: Single

Ages of children: N/A

Details of disabilities or serious illnesses:

Do you hold a current driving licence? No	Details of any endorsements: N/A
Do you own a house? No	Do you own a car? No

Leisure activities: Playing football

Next of kin: Mr/Mrs/Miss/Ms Brown

First name(s): John James

Relationship: Good

Address:

Education (Schools, Colleges, Universities): Gimchurch School, Gimchurch Middlesex
Blank Technical College, Finstone, Middlesex

Qualifications: GCSE English Lang (A) Maths (A) Geography (B) French (C) Biology

Referees: (Give names and addresses):

Mr J Smith Blank Technical College, Highway, Finstone, Middx, MX3 5DD

Mrs J Standing 25, South View, Gimchurch, Middx, NK12PT

Where John went wrong

◆ Has not used block capitals.

◆ First name(s): Has put first names in surname box.

◆ Address: Has not included the postcode.

◆ Date of birth: Has put current year instead of year of birth (this is a surprisingly common mistake).

◆ Place of birth: Should be Gimchurch, Middlesex.

◆ Nationality: Should be British.

◆ Details of disabilities or serious illnesses: Has left blank.

◆ Next of kin: Relationship should be 'Father'. Address has been omitted.

◆ Qualifications: Has omitted grade for biology.

Example 2: The right way

Bloggs and Bloggs Limited

Please return this application form to:
The Personnel Department, Bloggs and Bloggs Ltd, Gimchurch, Middlesex
Answer in BLOCK CAPITALS.
Confidential application for employment

Source of application: THE DAILY CHRONICLE	Date of application: 20 JUNE 2001

Post applied for: JUNIOR ACCOUNTS CLERK (REF A/JIC)

Surname: Mr/~~Mrs/Miss/Ms~~ BROWN

First Name(s): JAMES MICHAEL

Address: 25, THE MOOR, GIMCHURCH, MIDDLESEX, MX2 1 1E

Telephone number(s): 01765 43219 (DAY AND EVENING)

Date of birth: 1 JANUARY 1982	Place of birth: HARROW, MIDDX
Nationality: BRITISH	Marital Status: SINGLE

Ages of children: N/A

Details of disabilities or serious illnesses: NONE

Do you hold a current driving licence? NO	Details of any endorsements: N/A
Do you own a house? NO	Do you own a car? NO

Leisure activities: PLAYING FOOTBALL/ORNITHOLOGY/CINEMA

Next of kin: Mr/~~Mrs/Miss/Ms~~ BROWN

First name(s): JOHN JAMES

Relationship: FATHER

Address: 25 THE MOOR, GIMCHURCH, MIDDLESEX, MX2 1 1E

Education (Schools, Colleges, Universities): GIMCHURCH SCHOOL, GIMCHURCH MIDDLESEX
BLANK TECHNICAL COLLEGE, FINSTONE, MIDDLESEX

Qualifications: GCSE ENGLISH LANG (A) MATHS (A) GEOGRAPHY (B) FRENCH (C) BIOLOGY (C)
A-LEVELS TAKEN — AWAITING RESULTS: MATHS, APPLIED MATHS

Referees: (Give names and addresses):

MR J SMITH BLANK TECHNICAL COLLEGE, HIGHWAY, FINSTONE, MIDDX, MX3 5DD

MRS J STANDING 25, SOUTH VIEW, GIMCHURCH, MIDDX, NK12PT

Letter to accompany an application form

You should always send a letter to accompany an application form. The letter we used to reply to the sample advertisement on page 47 can be easily changed to suit this purpose. Simply rewrite the first and last paragraphs – then it does the job well. These could be rewritten along the following lines:

---

12 Sun Hill

Uckthorpe

Middlesex

MM2 0LJ

12 June 2001

Miss J Smith

Keystores

2 High Street

Uckthorpe

Middlesex

MM1 6QJ

Dear Miss Smith

Thank you for sending me the application form, which I have completed and have pleasure in returning to you together with my CV.

I leave school on 29 June and I could be available to start work immediately afterwards. If you wish to see me for an interview, I would be pleased to attend any day after 4 pm or earlier in the day if two days' notice is given.

Yours sincerely

Paul Page

Technology is going to play an increasing and inescapable part in the workplace of the future. The last few years have seen a significant increase in the use of electronic advertising for job vacancies and the facility for online job applications.

In the year 2000, a survey was carried out into the recruitment methods available for employers – such as external and internal advertising, personal contacts, careers days, recruitment agencies, etc. It showed that an astonishing **67 per cent** were already advertising job vacancies on the internet.

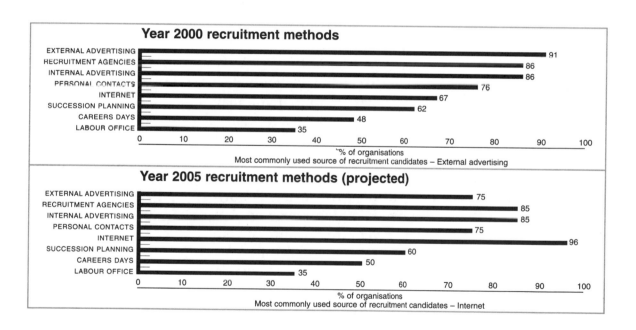

This trend is expected to continue and it is predicted that by 2005, 96 per cent of employers will be using the internet for recruitment and job advertisements.

All this has been made possible through advances in computer technology and the increased use of scanning software to read applications electronically.

You will find vacancies on both recruitment agencies' websites and on individual employers' sites. If you find a vacancy that is of interest to you on the internet, on either kind of site, you should consider applying electronically. Replying in the same medium says that you are comfortable with it. In addition, the employer may be looking for a quick response, or may want to get a feel for the quality of likely candidates, before they decide to advertise in the press. The organisation is also telling you that they are a company who uses the internet as part of their business process. Whatever the reason, you will have an opportunity to respond at an early stage of the selection process.

There are several advantages in applying electronically.

◆ It shows that you are computer literate.

◆ It shows that you are comfortable using the internet.

◆ You can be sure that your application will arrive on time and in perfect condition.

◆ It will give you the opportunity to demonstrate a skill and knowledge that the company may be looking for.

There is a disadvantage, too, however, in that you may be asked to reply to an advertised vacancy on a formatted form, normally an adapted version of the company's written application form. This form will have been designed to obtain standard and specific information about you and all you have to do is to fill in the blanks. The form will not allow you flexibility in presentation and you may not have enough space, within a box, to give a true picture of your skills, knowledge and ability. On the other hand, if your details are fairly straightforward, they are very convenient and may be worth using.

If you are required to apply by formatted application form, follow the same good practice as with a hard copy.

◆ Read the form and any instructions relating to it before you start. Many sites offer tips, hints and advice. This information can be very helpful, so make full use of it.

◆ Take your time, don't rush and consider your answers carefully before you enter them.

◆ Fill in all the boxes, inserting N/A if the section does not apply to you. Your application may be rejected if it appears that it is incomplete.

◆ Print off a copy of the form before you send it. This will enable you to assess how it looks as a hard copy.

If you apply online, be prepared to be asked also to complete an application form in hard copy at some stage during the selection process. This is to give the employer additional information about you and to assist them in assessing your written presentation skills.

Online CV applications

When compiling an electronic CV, your hard copy CV will prove useful as the same basic rules apply. However, an electronic CV has to adapted to the medium, and you should bear in mind the following rules.

◆ Keep it short.

◆ Keep it concise and relevant.

◆ Make it easy to read. Use standard fonts.

◆ Focus on your key skills, knowledge and /or career objectives.

As with any e-mail, you will have to fill in a subject line at the head of the application. Always fill in the subject line correctly and do not be tempted to put in a joke or something clever to attract attention. Do put in the job title and/or the reference number if there is one. If your application is speculative, put in a clear and concise statement to that effect.

Put your CV in the main body of the text, rather than sending it as a separate attachment. Organisations are sometimes wary of opening attachments because of viruses.

What should you include

Start with your electronic address i.e. your e-mail address. The date will automatically appear, but make sure it is correct and that your name is also shown at the top of the page.

Put your home address and telephone number at the **bottom** of the CV.

As with a hard copy CV, include your personal details, your personal statement, followed by your main skills, knowledge and/or experience, using the words and key phrases from the job advertisement in your application.

Make sure you include all relevant detail. For example, if the advertisement asks for 'a personnel officer with experience in all aspects of employment law including a knowledge of policies and procedures relating to a direct client workforce, experienced in building one-to-one relationships in a fundraising environment...', make sure the wording of your application reflects all of this.

Remember

Scanners are used to sift through most online applications. The scanner will be looking for key words relating to the position, i.e. marketing manager, administrator, research assistant, programmer, teacher, public relations, financial management, etc.

It will also be looking for a good match with the advertisement. Specifically, it will search for the skills and qualifications mentioned, such as 'experience of Microsoft Word/Excel'; 'NVQ Animal Care'; 'BSc/MA in ...'; 'record of achievement in policy development', etc.

It will look for particular words, such as organised, represented, managed, developed, implemented, designed and demonstrated, and phrases like 'the ability to write and present clear and persuasive reports'.

It will recognise phrases that indicate your occupational background, such as 'four years' experience in'; 'experience in writing reports that are clear'; 'ability to present the case persuasively'.

To demonstrate all of this, here are a sample online advertisement and application in response to it.

Example online advertisement

XXXXXX, a foremost charity in the field of XXXXXXX, operating in over 40 countries,

is seeking a

Volunteer Co-ordinator

to recruit and train our volunteers to support our work.

The successful applicant will have:

Experience of working with volunteers in third–world countries

Some knowledge of managing departmental budgets

They must also be:

Computer–literate, including use of the web

Self–motivated

Capable of bringing a creative dimension to the task, including the development of local strategies

Apply with CV etc.

Example online application

Subject: Volunteer Co-ordinator

Date: 2 June 2001

From: Your name, e-mail address

To: Company e-mail address

I am a highly self-motivated graduate with the ability to achieve results through working with people. I was involved in setting up a self-help group support team for homeless people, a job that included recruiting and organising volunteers. I managed the budget for the scheme. I am creative and enjoy a challenge.

Key skills

Here list your skills, giving IT ability first.

Budgetary skills

Include the value of any budget you handle, if you feel that it will benefit your case. If not, describe your responsibility, for example, in this case, 'budget responsibility for food and shelter'.

Career/work experience

Keep this section short but include dates.

Education

Again, make this brief, but include dates.

Personal details

Address:

Telephone number:

Interests

Complete this section as you would in a normal CV. Also include any further details that are requested, e.g. marital status, age, etc.

When you have applied for a job in response to an advertisement, you may receive a letter, inviting you to telephone for an application form or appointment. Sometimes you are given the option of telephoning or writing.

If you are given both options, I recommend telephoning if possible because it shows enthusiasm and confidence. It's a way you can chalk up some 'plus' points at a very early stage. Not only that, but there is also less chance that the job will be filled by someone else who reacts more quickly than you and has the offer of the job perhaps before your letter of application has had time to reach the company.

If possible, use a private telephone. Make sure you have enough space to take notes and make the call where you can be relaxed and undisturbed. If you are using a public telephone, be sure that you have enough money or units on your Phonecard for quite a long call.

Listen carefully to what is being asked of you. Speak clearly and not too quickly. Keep your answers brief and to the point. Avoid asking any more questions than are necessary. Your time to ask questions will come at the face-to-face interview.

Telephoning for an appointment

If you are invited to telephone for an appointment and not given the option to write, you can be fairly sure that the conversation will also involve a short interview, so be prepared to talk about yourself and the job.

Have the advertisement ready to hand with all the points underlined that have attracted you to the job and the specified requirements that you match.

Have your CV in front of you.

Have a diary ready to book the date of any appointment they may offer.

Have a note pad with written notes to act as memory-joggers during the conversation. The notes will include headings such as these:

- The company name
- The company telephone number
- The name of the person you have been asked to call
- Extension number of person you have been asked to call
- The job title
- Where the vacancy was advertised

Before you start the call, make notes about any other matters that may arise during the conversation. Put them under headings and number the points you want to think about. These may include:

- Why the job is interesting to you (look at your underlinings on the advertisement – pick up the points)
- Why the job is suitable for you (look at your underlinings on the advertisement – pick up the points)

During the conversation, make notes so that you will not forget what is said. Make sure you have the following information before you end the call:

- The date of your call
- The appointment – date and time
- ◆ The name of the person you are to ask for on arrival
- The address where the interview is to be held
- Any directions on how to find the company

Before you hang up, make sure that the company has your name, address and telephone number. Repeat back the date and time of the appointment.

Telephoning for an application form

This is likely to be a quick call to the person named in the advertisement. You should give your name, address, telephone number and the vacancy for which you are applying. It is probable that no further questions will be asked of you but be fully prepared just in case. You could find that the telephone call takes the form of a short interview, so make your notes as suggested before in 'Telephoning for an appointment'.

Before you pick up the phone, always check

◆ Have you got your notes?

◆ Do you have a note pad?

◆ Do you have a pen (which is working)?

◆ If calling from a public phone, do you have enough money or Phonecard units?

◆ Do you have the advertisement?

◆ Do you have your CV?

◆ Do you have a diary?

◆ Have you worked out exactly what you are going to say when your call is answered?

Telephoning to check on progress

Keep your application alive by regularly referring to your application file. If you find that you have applied for a specific vacancy and have not heard from the company within a couple of weeks of returning an application form, make a phone call to the person to whom you applied. Ask them politely if they have any news for you or when you might expect to hear from them. This kind of follow-up, approached in the right manner and spirit, can go down well. It indicates that you are seriously interested in the vacancy. However, you should **never** make your contact feel that you are putting pressure on them.

If your CV has been successful and you are offered an interview, you can feel justifiably proud of yourself. You have overcome the first hurdle. But now you need to look again at what you are trying to achieve and how you are going to achieve it, so that you make the best possible use of your interview opportunity. You need to be prepared to answer all the questions put to you, and also to ask questions of your own.

Memory-joggers

Write down a list of points that you hope to cover during the interview and notes on information you will hear during the interview and need to remember.

These will include some or all of the following. List them on the left-hand side of the page.

◆ The name of your interviewer(s)

◆ Their position in the company

◆ Further company information (about products/services, etc.)

◆ Any training provided

◆ Prospects

◆ Salary/holidays/hours of work

◆ Details of the next step in the selection process

◆ Anticipated starting date of successful candidate

Also write down any questions you think you may want to ask, such as:

◆ How has the position become vacant?

◆ Does the company have plans for future expansion?

◆ How will my performance be assessed?

◆ What are the long-term opportunities for promotion?

◆ What training will I be given?

◆ Do you encourage and further training and development?

- ◆ Do you fund it?
- ◆ How does this department fit in with the rest of the organisation?
- ◆ Who will I be working with?
- ◆ Will there be any further interviews for this position?
- ◆ When can I expect to hear your decision?

You could also add any technical questions appropriate to the post, such as, 'Which Windows package do you use?'.

Practise what you are going to say

You have thought about the questions you will be putting to your interviewer(s) and the impression you wish to make. But now think: 'What will they be trying to find out about me and what questions will they ask?'

Many questions can be anticipated in advance and it is wise to have some well-thought-out answers. Some interviewers use broad questioning techniques, such as 'Tell me about yourself', which can be extremely difficult to answer off the cuff. You need to be ready to offer the information you think that they want to hear.

Apart from a recognisable potential, with the specified qualifications and skill, they will also be looking for certain personal qualities that you possess. They will want to employ someone who is keen, hard-working and able to do the job. They will look for a sense of responsibility, honesty and loyalty. They will probably also want someone with acceptable social habits who can get on well with the other staff.

These are all important factors that contribute to your recognisable potential. Put simply, employers are always looking for the kind of person who will prove an asset to the company and whom they could proudly introduce as a member of their staff.

The questions that you could be asked to establish these objectives are potentially endless, but it is useful to think about and practise your response to questions like these:

- What do you know about us?
- What do you know about the vacancy?
- What experience do you have that relates to this job?
- Why are you interested in the job?
- Why are you looking to change your job?
- In what ways do you feel you are suitable for the job?
- Why did you apply for this post?
- In what way do think you can contribute to this company?
- Describe a difficult task you think you handled well and explain why.
- Describe a difficult task you did not handle well and explain why.
- What are your short-term/long-term goals?
- How would your boss/friend describe you?
- How do you work under pressure?
- In what kind of environment do you feel most comfortable?
- Are you pleased with your examination results?
- Why did you not do better in your examinations?
- What are the most valuable benefits you have gained from college/university?
- Have you made any decision you regret in your academic career?
- Have you responded well to the independence of university life?
- How do you get on with your contemporaries (classmates)?
- Do you read a newspaper? Which one?
- Why have you decided not to go on to further education?
- How did you get on with your teachers/tutors?
- What are your career objectives?
- What has been your greatest non-academic achievement?

- Would you have time for further study in the evenings?
- How would you travel to work if we offer you the job?
- Are you a good timekeeper?
- Do you think of yourself as a leader or a follower?
- Tell us about your leisure interests.
- Why should I employ you?
- Describe your strengths.
- What are you your weaknesses?

(These last two are typical of the tricky sort of questions that need plenty of thought in advance. Wherever possible, use your responses to describe aspects of yourself that could be of benefit to an employer. In the case of weaknesses, describe weaknesses that are disguised strengths, for example, not feel stretched or challenged. If you must describe a weakness, make sure it is something not relevant to the job. You could add that you tend to underestimate yourself.)

Having run through this list, you will no doubt be feeling that you are not quite perfect. However, in your conversation with your interviewer, always remember to highlight your strong points, your skills and good qualities and be reassured that no realistic manager is expecting to find total perfection in one human being.

Tips

If you are asked a 'sticky' question, don't let your mind scramble – buy yourself some time by repeating the question. For instance:

Interviewer: What has been your greatest non-academic achievement?

You: What has been my greatest non-academic achievement? Oh yes, it was when I won the …

However, you should only use this type of reply once, at the most twice, in the interview. Used more than that, it slows down the progress of the conversation and your interviewer will get bored and perhaps irritated.

Another way of dealing with an awkward statement or question from the interviewer is to answer it with a question followed by a countering positive. For example, you are applying for a vacancy for an Accounts Clerk:

Interviewer: You achieved only a low grade for your maths exam. Will your maths stand up in this job?

You: Do you think it is likely to be a problem? I have cashiering experience from working at Bloggs' Garage on Saturdays so I am not afraid of dealing with money and I do help my father with his book-keeping sometimes.

Again, you should not reply in this manner more than once during the interview. Bear in mind, too, that it is a response that needs putting over in a friendly way. It must not sound challenging. It is useful only if it is done well.

'Yes' and 'No' answers are absolutely fine, but do try to follow them by a relevant remark, albeit a short one. For instance:

Interviewer: Would you have any problems getting here if we gave you a job?

You: No. I have checked and there are two buses that are on the right route and would get me here in plenty of time.

A note on bluffing

The interview is your chance to convince an employer of your interest and enthusiasm, ability and desire to do the job. A little bluff to demonstrate your self-confidence is not a bad thing as long as you do not overdo it. However, modesty usually goes down better than arrogance and the line between confidence and arrogance is quite thin, so beware of going over the top.

More practical matters

There are also a few practical preparations to be made, so that there is no last-minute panic.

Getting there

Think carefully about how you are going to get there. It is important that you are not late. If you are travelling to your interview by car, work out your route and take a map with you if you are unfamiliar with the area. If you are going by public transport, look at relevant timetables well in advance so that you know precisely which bus or train to catch. Decide exactly when you need to leave home in order to arrive with time to spare. Take some change or a Phonecard with you in case you have to phone the company if you are delayed on route.

Clothes

Decide in advance what you are going to wear. Play safe but wear clothes you feel good in. As with application letters, appearances matter: your clothes and general tidiness say a lot about you and reflect your personality, so you should always look as though you have made an effort. If you have a suit, wear it. If not, wear an outfit that can be described as middle of the road; don't wear anything too casual (jeans are definitely not the thing) or too flamboyant in colour or style. Check your clothes over and make sure they are clean and well pressed. Make sure that your shoes and fingernails are clean too. Go easy on the perfume or aftershave.

What you need to take

Gather together everything that you will need for the interview and transfer it all to a separate file, bag or case. If you are using your old school bag or case, make sure it's in good condition. Do not use a plastic carrier bag.

Make sure that you have:

◆ The original advertisement

◆ The job description (if provided)

◆ Your CV

◆ A copy of the application letter

◆ Your telephone notes (if any)

◆ The letter asking you to attend the interview

◆ The company address and telephone number

◆ Company literature/information that you have compiled or they have sent to you

◆ Copies of your examination certificates

◆ Maps/timetables/directions on how to get there

◆ A note of the name of the person to ask for when you arrive

◆ Two pens

◆ A note pad with your memory-jogger notes (see page 73)

Ready to go

You have your file or bag ready with everything you need for your interview in it. You know how you are travelling to your interview and what time you need to leave home. You know what you are going to wear and you have checked that your clothes are clean and well pressed. And you have thought out some answers to some likely questions. So now relax, get an early night, and wake up feeling positive and sharp-witted.

Types of interview

Interviews come in various forms and the more you know about each kind, the better prepared you will be to perform well.

One-to-one interviews

These are usually formal, in-depth interviews in which you will meet just one interviewer, or several, one at a time. Typically, you will be interviewed by a human resources manager, or personnel officer or manager, and then go on to an interview with the manager of the department you will be employed in, or sometimes vice versa. If you are lucky, you will have both interviews on the same day, but there are occasions when you will be invited to return for the second interview.

Interview panels

These take the form of a meeting with several interviewers who will usually take turns to ask you questions. This can be rather daunting at first, but you will get used to it after a few minutes. When you first enter the room, you will probably exchange a few pleasantries with the members of the panel – try to take in their faces individually and you will soon start to relax. Make a point of addressing your answer to the member of the panel who puts the question to you; look at him or her while you speak and then acknowledge the other members at the end of your answer.

Group interviews

These take the form of a debate with other candidates. You will be given a topic to discuss and a company observer will assess your ability to communicate, your behaviour and your contribution to the proceedings.

Walk-in interviews

These can be fun if you are prepared to be patient. They are usually staged at a venue off the company premises, perhaps at a hotel. The 'just turn up' approach is used to speed up the recruitment process and attract a greater number of applicants. Companies find them useful when they have several jobs to fill. They are informal, relaxed occasions where you will be saturated with information and coffee but it may be a while before you actually meet an interviewer. You will have a short interview and, if you express interest in the position, you will either be given an application form or you may be booked in on the spot for a formal interview on the company premises.

Assessment tests

Designed to be fun to do, these are becoming increasingly used for recruitment purposes, in conjunction with the interview process. If you are prepared for them, there is no reason why they should throw you off-balance. It should be remembered that they are generally used to serve merely as an indicator of your suitability for the job. There are various types of tests designed for different purposes.

Skill tests

These demonstrate your level of ability in the skills you are offering, e.g. typing speeds.

Aptitude tests

These measure potential suitability for a type of work, e.g. dexterity for assembly jobs.

Knowledge tests

These give insight into the level of general knowledge of candidates in subjects related to particular jobs.

Intelligence tests

These are used to establish a candidate's powers of reasoning and logic.

Personality tests

These give insight into an applicant's motivations, strengths and weaknesses. They are commonly used in recruiting graduates and management and sales staff.

A word about interviewers

The interview is a two-way exchange of information for the purpose of establishing whether you are the right for the job and the job is right for you. You are there to learn about the company and in order to do this and to give a good performance, you need to be able to communicate well with the person who is interviewing you.

Every interviewer has his or her own style and it is worth bearing in mind that some interviewers are more experienced than others. Quite often you will find that the least experienced among them will conduct the least formal interviews. This may sound fine but be careful. They may mislead you unintentionally by their apparent enthusiasm at the interview, only to disappoint you later. The more experienced interviewers are masters at giving little away, so that you will leave with few or no clues as to your chances. This is because they are consciously keeping an open mind until they have seen everyone. Whatever form the interview takes and in whatever style it is conducted, the object of the exercise is to employ the right person for the job.

On the day

This is what you have been working and waiting for. It's the job you want – so go for it!

Make sure you are suitably dressed and have everything with you that you need (see pages 78–9). Arrive for your interview a little before time. Try to feel and look relaxed and cool – this will help to chalk up extra 'plus' points before the interview has even started. Think positive: you not only want the job but intend to be offered it. You may be feeling nervous – but who wouldn't be in the situation? If you are afraid that your nerves will show, don't worry, as you will find that you will relax increasingly as the interview progresses. An interview is an experience you should expect – or at least try – to enjoy.

Take a deep breath and walk into the offices confidently, ready to clinch a job offer.

Report to Reception and give them your name, the name of the person you are seeing and the appointment time.

Before you go in

While you are waiting, sit down if invited, and take in your surroundings. Have a quick scan through any company literature that might be lying on the table in the reception area. It is worth bearing in mind that some employers will check back with Reception about your arrival conduct.

Your interviewer may come to Reception to meet you or another member of staff may be sent instead. Whoever it is, stand up when they walk over to you and be ready to shake hands. Let them extend their hand first. Smile. Ask if you should take your coat with you or if there is anywhere they would like you to leave it.

The interview session

When you arrive at the interview room door, if you are entering alone, knock and then walk straight in. Once you have entered, don't just head for the nearest chair – wait to be invited to sit down.

If you are introduced to several interviewers, try to remember their names and their job titles. You probably will find that one person makes a point of taking charge of the proceedings. They will make the introductions and will indicate a chair for you to sit down on. Smile while the introductions are being made.

Sit tidily, upright or slightly inclined forward. Put your file on your lap. If you have a bag, place it on the floor by your chair. Do not put anything down on the interviewers' desk unless you are invited to do so.

Take out your CV and notes.

If you are asked if you would like a cup of tea or coffee, or any other kind of drink, accept it only if you really would like one (say something like, 'Yes please, if it's no trouble'). If your nerves are making you feel awkward and a bit clumsy, it is better to refuse politely. Cups can be difficult to handle when you have shaky hands and a lap full of papers.

Take note of your surroundings but keep alert and concentrate on what is being said. Do not be distracted by your interviewer's face or mannerisms. Remember to control your own movements – do not fiddle with jewellery or clothing.

Do not avoid eye contact – a little sparkle can work wonders. Interviewers can be nervous as well and it helps to relax everyone.

If you are asked if you would like a cigarette, always decline the offer (with thanks), even if you do smoke.

Answer everything as clearly and confidently as you can muster. (Refer back to pages 74–7 for ways to handle different questions.) When you get on to the subject of qualifications, ask if they would like to see your certificates.

It is possible that the interview may be interrupted by someone coming into the room or a telephone call being put through to your interviewer. If this happens, you should appear patient and discreet. Do not 'earwig', but use the time to look around you and take in your surroundings. Don't sigh, stretch or look bored. The interviewer may be irritated at the interruption, or it may have been stage-managed, but in either case your reactions will be noted.

Once your interviewers have completed their questions, they will probably ask if there is anything further you wish to know. Glance at your memory-jogger notes if necessary, but do not spend ages reading through them. By the end of the interview you should have been told all that is necessary about the company and the job to make your decisions about them. For the interviewers' part, they will have expected you to have been equally open about yourself so that they can make their decision about you.

Be ready for the signals to leave. Typically, these include your interviewer putting down their pen and tidying up papers that relate to the interview. They may lean back in their chair. They may look at their watch. Their closing phrases are likely to be: 'Thank you for coming to see me today' or 'We will be in contact with you over the next few days.' Take these as closing statements and actions, and prepare to leave. Do not try to prolong the interview.

Ending your interview

When you are sure the interview is over, shake hands with the interviewers and thank them for their time. Tell them that you have found the interview very interesting. If you have decided that you want the job, leave them in no doubt that it is a job you would like to do. Say so.

As you prepare to leave the interview room, try to orientate yourself again so you can set off down the corridor in the right direction. If you can't remember, simply turn and ask your interviewer, 'How do I find my way back to Reception?'. It's better than getting lost and feeling silly.

Leave the interview room as tidily and confidently as you came in. Take all your belongings with you.

Once you have left the interview room, under no circumstances should you go back for any reason whatsoever. If you suddenly realise that you have left something behind, ask a secretary or the receptionist to retrieve it for you.

If you are shown out by a member of staff, say goodbye and thank them. Say goodbye to the receptionist when you pass, if she is free. Be pleasant to everyone so they all feel that you are a nice person to have around.

As soon as possible after an interview, write down everything you now know about the job and company. Put down all the pros and cons, so that, if you are offered the job, you can see whether it's one that matches your requirements. Check whether there are any queries that you may need to put to the company before making your decision.

If it's a job that really appeals to you, it is a good idea to send a short letter to your interviewer at the company, thanking them for the interview and confirming your interest in the position. It should run something like this.

1 Valley Green
Strentham
Bucks
BU10 9LJ
8 June 2001

Mr R Fisher
Cam Engineering Ltd
Viking Way
Hornfield
Bucks
BU15 6QL

Dear Mr Fisher

Re: Your vacancy for an Accounts Assistant

I write to thank you for seeing me on 6 June.

I enjoyed my interview very much and I would like to confirm my interest in the job, which I feel is one that I could do well.

I look forward to hearing from you again soon.

Yours sincerely

John Smith

What next?

You are not quite home and dry yet. Even if you have left an interview convinced of your success and 100 per cent sure that you would like the job, you must now continue to look and apply for other vacancies. Keep yourself in a job-hunting routine and do not relax your efforts until you have a watertight offer in writing, giving the exact conditions of employment and salary. Even in what appears to be the most certain of cases, things can go wrong and once you have called a halt to your search, it is difficult to find the energy to start all over again. So keep going for the time being. Hopefully, within a very short time, you will have a choice of offers.

A job offer

So this is what it's all been about: you finally have an offer on your doormat. The letter should include information on the following:

◆ Your job title

◆ Your hours of work

◆ Your holiday entitlement

◆ Your salary and review periods

◆ The length of notice you have to give them should you wish to leave

◆ The length of notice they have to give you

Read it carefully and make sure you understand every point.

Alternatively, it may be a brief letter with a summary of the Terms and Conditions of Employment enclosed. This will provide all the statutory information that is required to be given within the first 13 weeks of your employment. However, in order to make your decision as to whether or not to take the job, you need all the information in the list above. If it is not included, telephone the person who sent the letter offering you the job, and ask for any additional information you require.

Assuming you are happy, write to the company immediately, giving your acceptance. As insurance, it is also a good idea to ring them and let them know that your acceptance is in the post. A letter of acceptance could be along these lines:

> 1 Valley Green
> Strentham
> Buckingshire
> BU10 9LJ
> 14 June 2001
>
> Mr R Fisher
> Cam Engineering Ltd
> Viking Way
> Hornfield
> Bucks
> BU15 6QL
>
> Dear Mr Fisher
>
> Re: Your vacancy for an Accounts Assistant.
>
> I am writing to thank you for your letter of 12 June offering me the position of Accounts Assistant.
>
> I am pleased to accept your offer and I look forward to starting work with you on 2 July 2001.
>
> Yours sincerely
>
> John Smith

Always keep the offer letter safe and keep a copy of your acceptance.

Having accepted a job, do not forget to cancel any outstanding appointments for interviews with other companies. In the excitement of your success, this may easily slip your mind, but it is important that you do it.

When you don't get the job

Unfortunately, you have to expect some turndowns and silences from companies. Taking 'No' for an answer is always hard but you have to be prepared for some negative outcomes. This is particularly likely if you have tried the speculative approach with your applications, where, to a great extent, success is just the luck of the draw. The right job being available at the right time for you is also a matter of luck. However, if after a reasonable time and a number of applications you are receiving only rejections, there must come a point when you have to ask yourself 'Why?'. If this happens to you, ask yourself these questions.

◆ Am I applying for the wrong jobs?

◆ Is my approach to my applications somehow wrong?

◆ Could my CV be improved?

◆ Am I projecting myself badly at interviews?

Having asked yourself these questions, if you do not come up with any useful answers, you should talk everything through with people whose opinions you respect. The most obvious will be your careers advisers but the views of family and friends can be very helpful too. It may be that you are doing all the right things and it is just a matter of bad luck so, if you continue as you are, the right offer will come you for you before long. On the other hand, they may be able to help you throw some light on where you're going wrong.

Conclusion

The way to success in finding a job is by identifying your skills and qualities and matching them to the opportunities right for you. You must be determined and organised and market your potential in the right way. Most of all, you have to play to win if you are to get anywhere. I hope the information in this book has gone some way to providing a positive, step-by-step guide to job-hunting, and that you will soon have a job to look forward to starting. If you have done everything suggested in this book, then you deserve to be a winner and, with time, you will be!

Some sources of information were mentioned in Step Two. This section gives fuller details of sources to help you find exactly what you need.

National Newspapers
The Daily Telegraph
    Thursday: All appointments
The Guardian
    Monday: Creative, Marketing, Media, Sales, Secretarial
    Tuesday: Education
    Wednesday: Environment, Health, Housing, Public
    Thursday: Computing, IT, Science, Technology
    Saturday: Commercial, Graduate
The Independent
    Monday: Computing, Graduate
    Tuesday: Marketing, Media, Health, Sales
    Wednesday: Financial, Legal
    Thursday: Graduate, General, Public
    Sunday: General
The Times
    Tuesday: Legal
    Wednesday: Administrative, Computing, Marketing, Media, Sales,
      Secretarial
    Thursday: Administrative, General, Public, Secretarial
    Friday: Education
    Sunday: Education, Executive, Public

Local newspapers
Find out the days when appointments are published. Note that some regional papers publish regional job supplements.

Careers guides
Your local library and Jobcentre will have copies of careers guides.

Training councils
The Training and Enterprise Council (in England and Wales) and the Local Enterprise Councils (in Scotland) work with employers to provide training opportunities and business and enterprise services. They are listed in the phone book.

Jobcentres
Jobcentres have a huge range of resources available for anyone looking for a job or information about employment. Your local Jobcentre will be listed in the phone book and should be able to provide the following:
● Lists of local job vacancies
● Information on local and national training schemes
● Information on local recruitment drives by particular employers
● Details of local recruitment agencies
● Local and possibly national newspapers appointments sections (some of this may be held on computer – ask the staff to help you)

The Internet
There is lots of career advice and information on the Net and more and more employers are advertising their vacancies on special websites – over two thirds at the most recent count. Finding them may not be easy. Here is a selection of useful website addresses to get you started.

- www.Cvsearch.net

Enter your CV on this site and they will put you in touch with employers whose requirements match your experience and qualifications. You can also receive details of jobs by e-mail.

- www.hobsons.co.uk

This is the premier site for details of thousands of career and education opportunities in the UK and around the world. Hobsons is a British and US-based company with over 25 years' experience in publishing educational and recruitment guides for young people.

- www.reed.co.uk

An effective site in which you can store employment opportunity details and link your requirements to specific jobs. A huge range of careers are covered, from junior to executive level. It offers regular e-mail updates.

- www.graduatebase.com

If you're a graduate and don't really know your next step, this site is packed with information on career options and how to choose them, plus interactive tools, interview tips and a jobfinder.

- www.jobserve.com

This site lists requirements sent in daily by IT recruitment agencies all over the UK and Europe. The details are entered into a database that can be sent out by e-mail to anyone who wants it. The site is based in the UK but often includes overseas vacancies.

- www.jobshark.co.uk

Here you can search for jobs, register your CV to receive e-mails about suitable jobs, or find useful information on job-hunting and the companies using the serve. Employers can register to receive CVs that match specific requirements. The service is part of a worldwide network – ideal if you are looking for a job abroad.

- www.milkround.com

This is an interesting and useful site providing details for graduates looking for work. It's quick to access, with a database to store your CV and send it to companies.

- www.jobsite.co.uk

Jobsite was created in 1995 and is the longest-established multi-sector Internet recruitment platform in the UK. It attracts hundreds of thousands of candidates every month from all industry sectors, including sales, marketing, management, accountancy, secretarial and administration, as well as IT, telecommunications and engineering.

- www.careers.lon.ac.uk

This comprehensive site is run by the University of London but would be useful for anyone whether they intend to go to university or not. It contains a virtual careers library that directs you to many resources. The topics covered include career choice, further study and job-hunting resources, professional bodies and employer websites.

- www.jobsearch.co.uk

This site covers a wide spectrum of fields of employment in the UK and is a good starting point.

- www.rileyguide.com

This is a directory of links to job-hunting resources from around the world, including job listings, CV and interview techniques, how to organise your job search, etc. It contains tips on how to use them and the information is comprehensive but there is rather a lot of text to read through, so while useful it is not a quick-search tool. It is, however, highly regarded and recommended even by other job site owners.

- www.thisislondon.co.uk

Although mainly London-based, this site gives details of training opportunities UK-wide, plus a CV composition section.